The Great Plague of London: The History and Legacy of England's Last Major Outbreak of the Bubonic Plague

By Charles River Editors

A medieval illustration depicting people with the plague being blessed

About Charles River Editors

Charles River Editors is a boutique digital publishing company, specializing in bringing history back to life with educational and engaging books on a wide range of topics. Keep up to date with our new and free offerings with this 5 second sign up on our weekly mailing list, and visit Our Kindle Author Page to see other recently published Kindle titles.

We make these books for you and always want to know our readers' opinions, so we encourage you to leave reviews and look forward to publishing new and exciting titles each week.

Introduction

A medieval depiction of plague victims being buried

The Great Plague of London

"The trend of recent research is pointing to a figure more like 45–50% of the European population dying during a four-year period. There is a fair amount of geographic variation. In Mediterranean Europe, areas such as Italy, the south of France and Spain, where plague ran for about four years consecutively, it was probably closer to 75–80% of the population. In Germany and England ... it was probably closer to 20%." - Philip Daileader, medieval historian

In the 14th century, a ruthless killer stalked the streets of England, wiping out up to 60% of the terror-stricken nation's inhabitants. This invisible and unforgiving terminator continued to harass the population for hundreds of years, but nothing could compare to the savagery it would unleash 3 centuries later. This conscienceless menace was none other than the notorious bubonic plague, also known as the "Black Death."

The High Middle Ages had seen a rise in Western Europe's population in previous centuries, but these gains were almost entirely erased as the plague spread rapidly across all of Europe from 1346-1353. With a medieval understanding of medicine, diagnosis, and illness, nobody understood what caused Black Death or how to truly treat it. As a result, many religious people assumed it was divine retribution, while superstitious and suspicious citizens saw a nefarious human plot involved and persecuted certain minority groups among them.

Though it is now widely believed that rats and fleas spread the disease by carrying the bubonic plague westward along well-established trade routes, and there are now vaccines to prevent the spread of the plague, the Black Death gruesomely killed upwards of 100 million people, with helpless chroniclers graphically describing the various stages of the disease. It took Europe decades for its population to bounce back, and similar plagues would affect various parts of the world for the next several centuries, but advances in medical technology have since allowed researchers to read various medieval accounts of the Black Death in order to understand the various strains of the disease. Furthermore, the social upheaval caused by the plague radically changed European societies, and some have noted that by the time the plague had passed, the Late Middle Ages would end with many of today's European nations firmly established.

In the mid-17th century, the heart of England fell victim to the mother of all epidemic catastrophes. The city of London was a ghost town, deserted by those who knew better than to hang around in a breeding ground that offered near-certain doom. Those who were confined within the city's borders had to make do with what they had, and the pitifully low morale seemed appropriate; the reek of rot and decomposition pervaded the air day in and day out, while corpses, young and old, riddled with strange swellings and blackened boils, littered the streets. For Londoners, to say it was hell would be an understatement.

The Great Plague of London: The History and Legacy of England's Last Major Outbreak of the Bubonic Plague explores the horrific disaster, its origins, the peculiar precautions and curious cures designed to combat the disease, and the sobering legacy it has left behind. Along with pictures depicting important people, places, and events, you will learn about the Great Plague of London like never before.

The Black Death

"Ring around a rosie, a pocket full of posies. Ashes, ashes, we all fall down." Oftentimes, giddy children can be seen belting out this jaunty, easily recognizable Mother Goose nursery rhyme, their hands linked as they dance around in a circle. As soon as the last word is uttered, the breathless children collapse in a fit of giggles. Bearing this in mind, many have since suggested that this iconic nursery rhyme is inlaid with nefarious undertones, and originated from even darker beginnings. According to a few chin-strokers, this seemingly innocent ditty was written as a morbid tribute to the merciless plague that ravaged Europe in the Middle Ages, lasting well into the 17th century.

Every line of the rhyme has since been dissected and extensively analyzed. For starters, a "rosie" referred to the middle portion of the back of one's hand, or the smooth space between one's wrist and fingers. Thusly, "ring around the rosie" was thought to be a romanticized description of the "rosie-red" or violet-tinged patches of rashes that appeared on the skin. This was one of the first tell-tale signs of the bubonic plague.

A "posie" was an old-fashioned term for "flower." This was said to describe the sprigs of flowers people had uprooted and either stuffed into their clothes or inhaled throughout the day, both a cost-effective and superstitious approach to staving off the disease. Others say it was used to mask the putrid scent of death from the mountains of disease-riddled bodies everywhere.

The definition behind the second line of the rhyme was varied. Some said it represented the flowers the dead were buried with, or had placed on their graves. There were also those who regarded the line as a visual depiction of the gut-churning pus that accumulated within the sores of the sick.

The "ashes" in the song signified the remnants of the diseased bodies, which were set ablaze to prevent the mysterious disease from multiplying. The ashes could also have signified the debris that remained from the houses that were torched to the ground, which had been ordered in response to the plague. In another version of the rhyme, "ashes" is replaced with "a-tishoo," the onomatopoeic term for a sneeze, and another common symptom of a certain strain of plague. Lastly, the final line of the rhyme and cue to the children's playful tumble to the ground was a reference to the swift and almost certain death that befell the ill-fated who were infected by the swift-acting contagion.

Today, theories of hidden meanings behind the nursery rhyme have generally been flushed down the drain by many historians, as well as the online myth-buster, *Snopes*. The rhyme first debuted in print in 1881, seen in *Mother Goose or the Old Nursery Rhymes*. Rumors suggested that the rhyme had been sung by children generation after generation since Europe's first tango with the plague, but there has been no record of the rhyme prior to the 1881 publication.

Multiple versions of the song were soon published thereafter. One alteration read, "Round the ring of roses, pots full of posies, the one stoops the last, shall tell whom she loves best." Another version recounts the posies being distributed to characters named Jim, Jack, and Moses. Contrarians hope to nip these theories in the bud, and have concluded that these versions, which clearly have nothing to do with death or disease, are simply a nonsensical song meant for the playground.

Nonetheless, what is certain is that the plague was a monstrous malady caused by the bacterium, *yersinia pestis.* The microscopic but lethal entity was usually fostered in the nests of wild rodents in sewers, streets, alleyways, and the squalid homes of the poor, and was believed to have multiplied with each furry body. Scientists today have coined names for these hotbeds of diseases – "plague reservoirs," or "plague focuses."

The plague comes in 3 strains – the septicemic, the pneumonic, and the bubonic. The septicemic plague is spawned when the aforementioned bacteria finds its way into the victim's bloodstream. The pneumonic is the deadliest of all the strains, as it seizes control of one's lungs. The invisible bacteria ejected from an ostensibly small cough or sneeze is enough to transmit the contagion to the next healthy person.

However, the most notorious strain is the bubonic plague, the first phase and most commonly contracted type of this disease. For many years, scientists have believed that the Black Death was a form of the bubonic plague, a deadly illness carried and spread by fleas found on rodents. The belief was that rats covered with the fleas traveled west on boats to Europe, where they reproduced and spread their infected parasites to humans, who subsequently contracted the plague and died. However, given the different strains and symptoms found across Europe, it has been alternatively suggested that the Black Death that attacked Europe during the 1340s and 1350s might also have been caused by an airborne pathogen of some sort, and this was certainly the belief that those afraid of the disease embraced. Gabriele de' Mussis, a lawyer in Piacenza during the Middle Ages, noted, "As it happened, among those who escaped from Caffa by boat were a few sailors who had been infected with the poisonous disease. Some boats were bound for Genoa, others went to Venice and to other Christian areas. When the sailors reached these palaces and mixed with the people there, it was as if they had brought evil spirits with them: every city, every settlement, every places was poisoned by the contagious pestilence, and their inhabitants, both men and women, died suddenly. And when one person had contracted the illness, he poisoned his whole family even as he fell and died, so that those preparing to bury his body were seized by death in the same way. Thus death entered through the windows, and as cities and towns were depopulated their inhabitants mourned their dead neighbors." Cortusii Patavini Duo, who wrote from Padua, recorded similar thoughts: "After which the unprecedented plague crossed the sea and so came to the Veneto, Lombardy, the March, Tuscany, Germany, France and spread through virtually the whole world. It was carried by some infected people who travelled from the East and who, by sight alone, or by touch, by breathing on them, killed everyone. The infection was incurable; it could not be avoided."

One of the things that made the plague seem to be some form of divine retribution is that it did indeed appear to have arrived from the East, a place the European Catholics considered pagan. Today it's apparent that the disease was not the result of an evil plot put together by the enemies of Christianity but almost certainly carried by rats infested with fleas. Still, many sailors returning to Europe from voyages to either Asia or the Middle East likely did bring the sickness with them, a fact that Mussis pointed out: "Thus almost everyone who had been in the East, or in the regions to the south and north, fell victim to sudden death after contracting this pestilential disease, as if struck by lethal arrow which raised a tumor on their bodies. The scale of the mortality and the form which it too persuaded those who lived, weeping and lamenting, through the bitter events of 1346 to 1348—the Chinese, Indians, Persians, Medes, Kurds, Armenians, Cilicians, Georgians, Mesopotamians, Nubians, Ethiopians, Turks, Egyptians, Arabs, Saracens and Greeks (for almost all the East had been affected)—that the last judgment had come."

While people struggled to explain the plague back then, today it is known that the plague is typically contracted by a pest, usually a rodent or a flea. In the most extreme cases, this brand of the disease can be incurred through the mere touch of an infected person's clothing. If untreated, which it almost always was, the disease would branch out to the blood or the lungs, which prompted the next phases of septicemic or pneumonic plague, respectively.

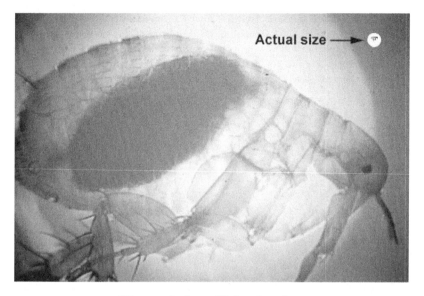

Actual size ⟶

Microscopic views of Oriental rat fleas

These days, when confronted with a mouse camping out behind a crack in the wall, or snacking on a treat in one's kitchen cupboard, most would squeal, make a snatch for the broom, and sweep them out the back door. In places with serious rodent infestations, people today often install mouse traps or resort to rodenticides to shoo away these pests, but back in the day, these privileges were far beyond the public's reach.

The disease was typically hosted by black rats, otherwise known as "ship rats" or "house rats." These critters were unlike the gray or brown rodents that frequented the nooks and crannies of cellars and sewers, often scurrying away at the sound of an approaching human's footsteps. It was precisely the black rat's habit of residing close to humans that made them such a menace to the public.

On average, it took about 10-14 days for a colony of the bacteria-infested rats to die out, but the decomposing rodents naturally attracted another swarm of fleas, on top of those that had already made permanent residence within the fur of these rats. These fleas, new and old, would become contaminated. Once the blood in these rodent corpses had been fully drained, the fleas would have no choice but to hunt for new hosts.

Infected fleas often set their targets on unsuspecting humans. Then, these fleas sunk their triple-probe mouth parts into the dirt-caked flesh of humans, most often dining in one's neck, armpit, groin, or thigh. Within a span of 3-5 days, the small, smarting bite would have ballooned into a tender, throbbing lymph node, known as a bubo, a term that later motivated the christening of the strain. When the infection had set in, the diseased faced an 80% mortality rate. From start to finish, their roller-coaster towards death came to a screeching halt in roughly 23 days. Apart from rats, other rumored carriers of the disease were cats, rabbits, squirrels, chipmunks, prairie dogs, and even house-broken pets.

A victim of the bubonic plague with swollen lymph nodes visible

A victim of the bubonic plague with fingers blackened by the illness

By the 17th century, the plague was a familiar anomaly to the people of Europe, for it was anything but their first kiss with the debilitating disease. The earliest case in Europe was reported to have occurred in Messina, Sicily, in October of 1347. A fleet of a dozen Genoese trading ships from the Crimean region were docked at the Sicilian harbor, seemingly taking a brief respite after lengthy and turbulent travels through the Black Sea. As they were expected to have embarked upon a trading route that took them past Constantinople, through the glittering green heart of the Mediterranean Seas and into China, the townspeople were excited to hear their exotic tales, and steal a peek at the porcelain, silk, and tea brought back from faraway lands. Crowds gathered around the ships to welcome the travelers, waving, cheering, and offering them well wishes. But this cheering soon petered out when the visitors noticed how strangely still these ships were. Not a single soul had come out to meet them. Spooked, a band of men dispatched from the local authorities boarded the ships to investigate the uncanny silence, only to be greeted by a hideous sight. In all 12 ships, all the crewmen were either slumped over against wayward furniture, or sprawled out across the floors. Most of them were ice-cold and perfectly rigid. Only a fraction remained breathing, but just barely.

More sweat coursed down the rattled investigators' necks when they saw that all the sailors exhibited the same eerie symptoms. Those clinging onto their last breaths were curled up in a ball, or doubled over in excruciating pain, their lips chalky-white, but their faces and skin hot to the touch. Most alarming of all were the ghastly black boils that had sprouted from these men's bodies, pulsing and oozing a nauseating mixture of pus and blood. These men rolled around, delirious, hallucinating, and clearly dehydrated, but what food and water they could manage immediately shot back out of them. It was these very boils that would give this dreadful condition its nickname – "black death."

It did not take long for the locals of Messina to realize the gravity of having readily invited a little-known but clearly deadly disease into their land. They quickly shunned the ships from the port, but the damage was already done. The plague spread through the city like an uncontainable wildfire. A great number of those who had been stricken tried to escape and sought refuge in the countryside, but that only carried the disease into rural Messina.

Pandemonium would not be a strong enough term to describe the chaos that had erupted. By the next month, the so-called "death ships" that were thrust back into sea were said to have randomly steered themselves into the docks of the Mediterranean islands of Sardinia, an autonomous region of Italy, and Corsica of France. Tana, a trading post in Genoa, Italy, became another breeding ground for the plague. The unforeseen outbreak was grave enough to interrupt a conflict between the Christian merchants and the Tatars, the latter a Muslim Turkic people who had taken control of the Christian stronghold in the Crimean city of Caffa.

Today, the short-lived invasion is known as the "Siege of Caffa," which was said to have featured one of the earliest instances of biological warfare. When the plague struck, the Tatars were forced to retreat, lest they be infected. Before doing so, they launched plague-claimed corpses over the wall in a last-ditch attempt to infect the residents. The citizens of Caffa hustled to fling these corpses out into sea, but the damage had been done. Thousands fell ill and later succumbed to the disease. A few attempted to book it, boarding ships and setting sail for neighboring countries. In the process, many of them unwittingly become carriers of the disease.

That was all it took for the plague to continue spreading. That year, only a few regions in Italy and Greece would feel the wrath of the plague, but that would soon change. In just another 6 months, about half the continent had been affected by the plague. Those in Marseilles, France, as well as Valencia and Barcelona of Spain, would meet a similar fate to those at Messina.

The plague was as ruthless as it was unstoppable. The absence of a proper international, or even cross-continental communication system made it even more difficult for the stricken cities to sound the alarm bells in time. In the months that followed, the disease with no bias seeped into the borders of Germany, as well as certain regions of Africa and the Middle East.

Italy ranked close to the top of the doom list. The plague had spread from Genoa to Tuscany, and from there to Florence, Siena, Rome, and Avignon, the papal city at the time. Florence suffered one of the worst mortality rates, seeing 100,000 of its inhabitants wiped out in the span of 4 months. In certain neighboring cities, the plague was said to have killed up to 90% of their residents.

When the disease reached Milan, authorities there were one of the first to enact preventative measures. As soon as the pestilence made an appearance in the city, claiming the inhabitants of the first 3 houses, said houses were instantly quarantined. Under instruction of the Milanese archbishop, the afflicted were locked in and kept under medieval house arrest, where they were essentially left with no other option but to await their impending deaths. As cold-blooded as the measure might seem, it appeared to be the only viable option in a panicking and primitive climate. It also seemed to bear fruit to some extent, as the city's mortality rates were visibly lower than those of their neighbors.

The streets of Florence experienced one of the most deafening silences, losing 65,000 of its citizens. Giovanni Boccaccio, author of *The Decameron*, painted a haunting picture of the scene: "In the year of our Lord 1348...in Florence, the finest city in all of Italy, a most terrible plague...Men and women in great numbers left the city, their houses, relations, and effects, and tied into the country...concluding that none ought to stay in a place thus doomed to destruction."

A depiction of the plague in Florence as described by *The Decameron*

A medieval depiction of Boccaccio and other Florentines fleeing the plague

In the city of Siena, the disease was taking a flagrant toll on everyday business. Construction on a cathedral ceased the moment the contractors were gusted with the frigid wind of disease. Funds for the project had to be diverted to the aid of the ill workers. Ultimately, the project was scrapped and the site left abandoned. It can still be found today, serving as a chilling reminder of the historic plague.

During this time, a group of God-fearing vigilantes took matters into their own hands. These men maintained a widely-held belief that the plague was a product of God's anger. Collectively known as the "Brotherhood of the Flagellants," the brothers marched through the cities of Europe, their pleading prayers ringing across the gloomy streets as they lashed at themselves with thorny scourges. At times, they invited passersby to join in on the act, a perfect example of the testament to the desperation of the tainted cities.

Over the next 5 years, an estimated 20-30 million perished in Europe alone. This sobering statistic would one day lead chroniclers to describe the event as the "medieval equivalent of a nuclear holocaust." As the plague secured most of the trade routes, avoiding the plague was next to impossible. The southern tip of England was infected as early as June of 1348, and by the next year, the disease had made its way through the rest of Great Britain.

Due to their limited knowledge of medicine, and the almost total lack of any reliable method of studying and treating disease, there were no verifiable ways known to avoid contracting the disease. As such, rumors began to spread abundantly. Louis Heyligen, a musician serving Cardinal Giovanni Colonna, hoped that maybe he had learned something while working in the papal court that could save his friends. In a letter, he wrote, "I am writing to you, most dearly beloved, so that you should know in what perils we are now living. And if you wish to preserve yourselves, the best advice is that a man should eat and drink moderately, and avoid getting cold, and refrain from any excess, and above all mix little with people—unless it be with a few who have healthy breath; but it is best to stay at home until the epidemic has passed. According to astrologers the epidemic takes ten years to complete its cycle, of which three have now elapsed, and so it is to be feared that in the end it will have encircled the whole world, although they say that it will affect the cold region more slowly."

On the other hand, Giovanni Boccaccio had his own ideas about what would prevent one from catching the plague, though since he was neither a doctor nor a scientist, his ideas were more of a hopeful collection of rumors going around than any sort of definitive advice. He wrote, "Some thought that moderate living and the avoidance of all superfluity would preserve them from the epidemic. They formed small communities, living entirely separate from everybody else. They shut themselves up in houses where there were no sick, eating the finest food and drinking the best wine very temperately, avoiding all excess, allowing no news or discussion of death and sickness, and passing the time in music and suchlike pleasures. Others thought just the opposite. They thought the sure cure for the plague was to drink and be merry, to go about singing and amusing themselves, satisfying every appetite they could, laughing and jesting at what happened. They put their words into practice, spent day and night going from tavern to tavern, drinking immoderately, or went into other people's houses, doing only those things which pleased them. This they could easily do because everyone felt doomed and had abandoned his property, so that most houses became common property and any stranger who went in made use of them as if he had owned them. And with all this bestial behavior, they avoided the sick as much as possible.

… Many others adopted a course of life midway between the two just described. They did not restrict their victuals so much as the former, nor allow themselves to be drunken and dissolute like the latter, but satisfied their appetites moderately. They did not shut themselves up, but went about, carrying flowers or scented herbs or perfumes in their hands, in the belief that it was an excellent thing to comfort the brain with such odors; for the whole air was infected with the smell of dead bodies, of sick persons and medicines."

There were a few portions of Europe that succeeded in avoiding the plague. Milan's brutal preventative measures proved effective, and it emerged as one of the cities with the lowest plague-induced mortality rates. Southern France, one of the lesser populated areas, as well as the port city of Bruges, managed to escape relatively unscathed.

Be that as it may, the plague would not stay away. Mass outbreaks would be resurrected, targeting different cities every couple of decades. It struck London again in 1349, where the city experienced nearly 3 consecutive outbreaks in the same year. Then, it revisited Paris in 1466, where 40,000 died in the city itself. In 1497, it would be Barcelona that was affected. Between the first plague pandemic and 1497, Barcelona, along with the Catalonian region, underwent a drastic shrink in population, with the census dropping from an estimated 600,000 to 278,000.

The plague persisted into the next century, ravaging Madrid in 1506, and Seville a few years prior, which claimed up to 700,000 lives. In 1550, the disease cut the population of York in half. Even Milan, which had succeeded in dodging the plague for so long, could not hold on much longer. In 1630, about 150,000 of its 200,000-250,000 inhabitants were no more.

An early 15th century Bible's illustration believed to depict the plague

That said, it seemed that none could compare to England, as the nation appeared to be an inauspicious magnet for the miserable disease. Following its first strike in the 14th century, the problem reached such a dire status that mass graves had to be shoveled out of the ground to accommodate the countless bodies. The city of London suffered a couple more times closely after, once in 1563, and then again in 1625.

The plague had become such a regular occurrence that authorities scrambled to contain the situation with laws, regulations, and decrees. In 1518, the first regulations were installed in London, requiring its citizens to hang a bundle of straw outside their door to signify an infected house. The infected would then be boxed into their homes for a period of 40 days. The infected were also tasked with carrying sticks dipped in white paint in the rare occasion they were allowed in public, so that others would know to keep their distance. The disease continued to linger, which resulted in more seemingly futile regulations.

In the summer of 1644, a fresh outbreak in Oxford, home to the king, reanimated the panic. More quarantines, as well as the mass slaying of cats and dogs, both wild and domesticated, were ordered. In Newark, guards were stationed by the doors of the quarantined homes, which did nothing to slow down the plague's effects. By 1646, following another 1,000 recorded deaths, Newark was labeled "a miserable stinking infected town." In the next year, another 3,597 plague-related deaths were recorded in London. As macabre as the figure sounds today, to the 17th century Londoners, this was a good year.

For reasons undisclosed to the residents, the city of London seemed to have been dealt one of the worst hands in the country – perhaps all of the continent. Time and time again, the city had been smitten with returning epidemics. In 1603, the plague claimed 30,000 lives. 22 years later, that number was bumped up to 35,000. Later on, Londoners were granted a glimpse of hope as that number dropped to 10,000 in 1636, and it continued to sink steadily lower after that. Londoners hoped that the dwindling mortality rates signified the dawn of a better day. Much to their consternation, it would be anything but.

One cold winter night in 1664, a bright, fiery comet hurtled across the inky night sky. This, the gasping witnesses believed, was an omen of doom and destruction. As it turned out, the worst epidemic was indeed lurking on the horizon.

The Roots of the Plague

"How many valiant men, how many fair ladies, breakfast with their kinfolk and the same night supped with their ancestors in the next world...Many died in the open street, others dying in their houses, made it known by the stench of their rotting bodies." – Giovanni Boccaccio

Even to this day, the origins of the Black Death are disputed. A wide range of historians have suspected and named China, India, Mongolia, as well as other parts of central Asia and southern Russia as the source of the crippling disease. While documents from the 14th century have presented theories relating to the disease's eastern origins, modern historians take this fact with a grain of salt, as none of these were first-hand accounts.

One of the most popular theories of origin blames China as the source of the plague, apparently making its first appearance over 2,600 years ago. These "oriental rat fleas" not only hitched a ride on critters that journeyed across the Silk Road, they became unwanted passengers on trading vessels. From that point forward, the disease was said to have bled into Western Europe around the 14th century, and later, to Africa. When the plague was introduced to the United States through Hawaii 500 years later, fingers were once again pointed at China.

In the early 2000s, archaeologist Eva Panagiotakopulu from the University of Sheffield, England, challenged this theory. The fossil expert declared that the plague had originated in Egypt, and she claimed that she had found archaeological evidence to support her theory. These findings had been discovered by chance during a routine excavation that aimed to learn more about the daily life of Egyptians 3 millennia ago. The dried up insects unearthed at the site, Panagiotakopulu insisted, were her golden clues. While sifting through the ruins of what had once been the homes of pharaoh tomb-makers, she had come upon the remains of both cat and human fleas. Mummified rats later found by the Nile Delta added weight to this theory. Most intriguing of all, ancient medical writings from a document entitled "Ebers Papyrus," circa 1500 BCE, described an all-too-familiar disease, one that "produced a bubo, and pus that [has] petrified."

The first of the 3 plague pandemics to come is now referred to as the "Justinian Plague," as it had occurred during the era of Byzantine Emperor Justinian the Great's reign (527-565). The first case of the destructive disease was recorded in Pelusium in the year 541, a city in Egypt's Nile Delta. Others claim the disease had made its first waves a year earlier in Ethiopia. From Pelusium, the plague split east and west, heading to the densely populated cities of Palestine and Alexandria.

By 544, the disease, which saw its victims conquered by buboes and septicemia, had penetrated the borders of the African Tunisia, and Italy. For the next 2 centuries, the areas of what would become England and Ireland, as well as the Sahara, Iberian Peninsula, Persia, and other stretches of east Asia would have their first encounters with the calamity. Between the years of 541 and 749, there were at least 17 different outbreaks around the globe.

Procopius of Caesarea, a Byzantine court chronicler, portrayed the plague as one powerful enough that the "whole human race came near to be annihilated." Excerpts from his book, *History of the Wars,* exhibited a vivid image of the events: "[The ill] were seized by the disease without becoming aware of what was coming, either through a waking vision or dream...They had sudden fever, some when just roused from sleep, others while walking about, and others while otherwise engaged, without any regard to what they were doing...In others on the following day, and in the rest not many days later, a bubonic swelling developed."

Not surprisingly, the mortality rates during the time are inconclusive. Between 541 and 544, the death toll had been placed at anywhere between 5,000-10,000. In Constantinople, home to Emperor Justinian, the plague victims died daily, claiming up to 300,000 lives at the end of its course. These virulent attacks and their frequent comebacks were rightly classified as "pandemics," as they affected a large portion of the world in a chain of cyclic infections.

But what could have brought about the second and third pandemics? The deplorable hygiene and sanitary conditions from the days of yore are believed to have been the chief contributors to the birth of the disease. Medieval sanitation in European cities, as opposed to the countryside, was especially abhorrent, due to its congested and poorly engineered towns, many of which were overrun by overpopulation. In a matter of 60 years, the number of citizens had tripled, with over half a million residents sandwiched within the city walls.

Rivers were not only a means of transportation, but served as the foundation for all basic necessities of the time. This was not only where the townspeople bathed, but where waste and garbage were disposed. Even so, people habitually filled their pails with the filthy river water, and, in a twist that would make modern health inspectors faint, they later used the water for cooking and drinking. The only semblance of a plumbing system consisted of the crude ditches and sewers that emptied out into the rivers.

In London, sanitary conditions were just as atrocious. Even in the homes of the wealthy, grimy chamber pots were stowed under beds for easy access to the toilet during the middle of the night. It is said that the British slang term for bathroom, "loo," had been birthed from the French term "*guardez le' eau*," which translates to "watch out for the water." Additionally, dirty leaves or moss were used as toilet paper.

Medieval Europeans were known for dumping their garbage and the contents of their chamber pots straight out of their windows and into the streets. Of course, before doing so, common etiquette required a trio of warning cries, so those outside could duck from the incoming splash in time. Some who had the room used chamber pots, and attached small rooms as an extension to their outermost walls on the second floor instead. There, a hole was punched into the ground of the private loo, designed so the user's waste flowed (or plopped) right into the alley or street below. Cesspits, which were holes dug out of the earth on their property, served as bathrooms for the poor. These were supposed to be regularly emptied, but this was rarely done.

Apart from the stream of excrement teeming through the town, the streets doubled as a landfill. Daily loads of garbage, along with entrails and discarded parts from the butcher shops, were also tossed out into the streets. Oftentimes, the blood-infused river of sewage spilled into the homes and nearby establishments around the butcher shops. To combat the rapidly mounting waste, townspeople relied on hungry animals and a rinse from the skies to drive the worst of the waste out of town.

In time, new technology and innovations sought to rectify the towns' hazardous conditions, but the tremendous ignorance of science made this an unachievable dream. This was a time when people were more than happy to apply leaded makeup to their faces, and swipe toxic powders and creams across their lips and eyelids. Scorching-hot pokers and leeches were the only available solutions for disinfecting a wound.

Beds were inhabited by bugs, pests, and at times, bird droppings, as most homes were built without roofs. Laundry detergent in ancient Rome consisted of lye made of ashes and urine, and even then, it was sparingly used. Medieval folk did not change their clothes, hats, or lice-infested wigs for months on end, as many believed that bathing was bad for one's health, a myth propagated by King James VI of Scotland himself.

King James VI of Scotland and I of England

By the time England had entered the 17th century, hygiene was no different, and in fact, some might say, was arguably worse. Though a hefty fine of 2 shillings had been placed upon those who were caught chucking garbage or excrement into the streets, few took heed of the new law. As pavements did not yet exist, people walked on the naked earth – in reality, the seemingly breathing tons of excrement, blood, and waste running through the winding streets. City sweepers, or "muck-rakers," were entrusted with scraping the filth off the streets, and since it was a job no one wanted, they were paid quite handsomely. The job was made even more unappealing by the fact that medieval Londoners and animals were said to have produced up to 50 tons of excrement every single day.

In poorer neighborhoods, sanitation was particularly difficult to police. Muck-rakers avoided the cities like the very disease that tormented them. As a result, the ground was constantly thick and slippery with waste and rotting carcasses, reeling in armies of resident flies and insects. When muck-rakers braved these neighborhoods, the waste from these cities would only be swept outside the city walls, where separate mounds of months' old waste were left to spoil even further. Day in and day out, people swerved out of the way to avoid getting drenched by irresponsible homeowners from the floors above, as well as the puddle splashes from carriages and horses whisking through the streets.

People did what they could to tolerate the noxious funk in the air. They walked around with handkerchiefs or "nosegays," which were satchels of flowers pressed firmly against their noses. The thick billows of black smoke coughing out of the 15,000 coal houses, along with the factories and breweries, made breathing even more challenging. Immigrants who had flooded the city in recent years had taken over massive tenements, which became vandalized, decrepit, and sordid, luring in even more rodents.

As 1665 rolled around, the bubonic plague had become a recurring nightmare that the people had grown accustomed to but did not understand. Scientists, scholars, and the greatest minds all tried to find a cure for the plague, only to find themselves defeated each time. The 14th century papal physician, Guy de Chauliac, put the shared sentiment into words: "The disease was most humiliating for the physicians, who were unable to render any assistance."

In England, the blame was blindly pinned onto an assortment of causes. Apart from divine intervention, the plague was believed to have been caused by certain planetary movements. Others claimed it had to do with the toxic fumes in the air. Then, there were those who theorized that their enemies had infiltrated their territory, poisoning the local wells to weaken its inhabitants. Some saw clues in the bad weather and their sick livestock, and found the abrupt explosion in the population of frogs, mice, flies, and other unwanted pests most suspicious.

Whatever the reason, the plague always loomed in the background, and in 1665, it would come back with a vengeance.

A Familiar Chaos

"We are all bound thither; we are hastening to the same common goal. Black death calls all things under the sway of its laws." – Ovid, Roman poet

One of the first signs that heralded the final wave of the third plague pandemic arose in December of 1664, not long after the seemingly portentous comet was sighted. The streets of London had only begun to simmer down when the grim tidings of the plague's return started to make its rounds. This red flag had been raised by a clergyman by the name of John Allen, who hailed from Amwell Street in London. One freezing night that winter, Allen popped into the Phillips residence for a visit. Allen was led up the creaking staircase and into the cluttered bedroom of the ill, a young, once fair maiden by the name of Mary, who had once been tried as a witch just a few years prior. The bedridden woman made no acknowledgment of the priest's presence, as she was much too preoccupied with writhing on the bed, her mind hopelessly lost in her restless, feverish state.

To Allen, these were the symptoms he had hoped he would never encounter again, but yet, here he was. Upon further inspection, an unmistakable boil the size of an apple was found protruding from the size of Mary's neck. He cringed as he watched the black and brown pus dribble out of the blistered bubo.

Allen stayed by Mary's side as her mother swept aside her scraggly, greasy hair, dabbing at the sweat trickling down her discolored face. The priest, who was certain the end was near, dutifully prayed with her for several hours, up until her last gasp of breath. Allen later wrote about the heartrending experience in a letter to his brother, lamenting, "In this fetid, grimy city, this poor soul departed this life in the greatest agony. She tossed and turned, this way and that, shouting for her deliverance. At 4 in the morn, the pestilence burst forth from the boils, destroying her at once."

Unbeknownst to the Londoners, the plague had made its stealthy return. A few at the time began to contemplate the "miasma" effect as a source of origin, suspecting the disease to be airborne. Apart from that conjecture, authorities were left baffled by the inexplicable terror that was the plague.

While Mary Phillips, along with a few other documented cases sprinkled around the city, were killed by the plague, the disease would not truly rear its head until a year later. Some today theorize its delay was brought about by the winter, and though these cases had ended in fatalities, the public had wishfully disregarded them as freak, one-off cases.

No one saw cause for alarm until the death of Rebecca Andrews. Rebecca was a resident of Cock and Key Alley, which belonged to the St. Dunstan's Parish by Fleet Street, one of the major streets in London. She lived amongst 30 other impoverished families of varying sizes, squeezed into a horridly crowded community with some of the foulest living conditions in the entire city. The local churchwarden, Henry Dorsett, oversaw the alley. The poor of Cock and Key held a special place in his heart, as he, too, had come from similar beginnings.

Rebecca, like her neighbors, was numb to the horrors of everyday life, and made do with what she had. She was fondly remembered for fostering orphans and disabled children running amok in the slums. At the time, she had taken in an abandoned boy named Laurence.

According to most sources, the date of Rebecca's death is listed as April 12, 1665. This was the same date another young woman by the name of Margaret Porteus succumbed to her infection. Porteous was later buried in Covent Garden, located south of St. Giles-in-the-Fields, just half a mile away from Cock and Key Alley.

Other sources, including the Channel 4 film documentary, *The Great Plague*, placed Rebecca's date of death on the 15th of June. The same film named Rebecca as patient zero of Cock and Key Alley, unknowingly signing the death warrants of the tiny community. A local physician had been sent over to her home, where he found her frail, barely-breathing body in the corner of the room. The instant the physician's eyes landed on the overt boil under her arm, the shade of his face matched her sickly primrose complexion. There was no denying it – Rebecca Andrews had the plague.

Authorities ordered for Rebecca's house to be sealed shut at once. She was quarantined alongside Laurence, who, upon the physician's first visit, had not yet displayed any symptoms of the disease. Still, a blacksmith was hired to attach a heavy padlock onto the front door. Planks of wood were nailed to all the doors and windows, leaving the widow and the orphan in a pitch-black vacuum of a prison. Neighbors took turns guarding the door to ensure that Laurence did not escape, as well as to prevent unapproved visits. About a week later, nurses returned and found Rebecca's limp body. Laurence might still have been blinking, but a boil had formed under his chin. Within the next 24 hours, the boy passed on, finally put out of his misery.

When signs of the plague began to crop up in various areas around London, people had no choice but to face the music. Another notable case was recounted in the diary of Samuel Pepys, an administrator in the English Navy and Member of Parliament. Pepys, most known for his religious journal writing, kept up his regular logging for over a decade. In his now celebrated and often referenced work, he recounted the savagery of the outbreak.

Pepys

On the 24th of July, the parish of Saint Olave Hart Street announced the death of Mary Ramsey, an indigent young girl who resided with her family in the spare room of a beggarly almshouse. This would be the first plague-related death recorded in this parish. The death of young Mary had come as a double-whammy for the Ramsey family, for her sister had been laid to rest just a day before, albeit from unrelated causes. A day after Mary Ramsey's death, another boy who shared a room with the Ramseys also died from the plague and was buried alongside them.

Accounts at the time asserted that it was Mary Ramsey who had brought the plague to London with her from France, where she was thought to have previously resided up to the early 1660s. Modern historians beg to differ; instead, they speculate that the disease had traveled all the way from the Netherlands. The Netherlands had always been a hub for the plague, so much so that its residents' leading causes of death had been marked by the disease since 1599. Dutch trading ships bearing cargoes of cotton from Amsterdam are said to have been the culprits, as the city had suffered an egregious outbreak between 1663 and 1664, losing up to 50,000 of its inhabitants. Upon realizing this, King Charles II of England canceled all trade with the Dutch in an effort to avert the disease's path, but by then, the king was powerless to stop it.

King Charles II of England

There remains considerable disagreement concerning the trigger to this vicious outbreak, mainly due to the inconsistency of the Bills of Mortality. These bills had been issued by Parliament in November of 1532, and were the equivalent of death certificates. Initially, these were strictly designed to keep track of the plague mortality rates in different parishes, and the practice of weekly transcriptions only began during the brief outbreak in London between December of 1592 and December of 1595.

The Bills of Mortality were retired fleetingly, but they were soon brought back during yet another outbreak in 1603. From then onward, it was used to record all the weekly deaths of each parish. An initial or symbol next to the name of deceased was added to these bills to indicate their cause of death. For the English parishes in the 1660s, these bills were inundated with name after name, almost all of which had the letter "P" next to them. As the outbreak persevered, these names were reduced to impersonal descriptions such as "boy," "girl," or "man in the street," as the bill writers could no longer keep abreast of the nonstop deaths.

A Bill of Mortality for 1665

John Graunt, a well-to-do merchant with a passion for science and an honored member of the Fellowship of the Royal Academy, was one of the first to be entrusted with the record taking for these bills. As these bills were penned by different parishes and later compiled into one antiquated and heavily insecure database, certain missing dates, figures, and gaps in these logs remain unsolved. The irregularities of the record-keeping made it even trickier to properly identify the patient zeroes of any particular outbreak.

In July of 1665, the public of London found themselves backed into a corner, forced to stare the facts they had neglected – perhaps intentionally – to take seriously. The plague had returned in its full force. King Charles II and his entourage, foreseeing the threat, loaded up their carriages and made off for Salisbury, and later to Oxford.

Those who could afford it –wealthy merchants, lawyers, and other higher-ups in society – scooped up their families and left town. In October, Parliament also decided to make themselves scarce, rehousing in Oxford, where they joined the king. Packs of clergymen who elected to serve the community in spirit joined the refugees. Most of the doctors, including the College of Surgeons, declined to stay behind to look after the plague-stricken and instead hightailed it to the countryside.

All in all, an estimated 200,000 people deserted the city. Daniel Defoe, author of *Journal of the Plague Years*, explained the scene: "Nothing was to be seen but wagons and carts, with goods, women, servants, children, coaches, filled with people of the better sort, and horsemen attending them, all hurrying away."

Defoe

Among the braver souls who opted to forgo the disappearing act were a few dozen sheriffs, aldermen, and leaders of parishes. Perhaps most noteworthy of those who had stayed put was the Lord Mayor of London, Sir John Lawrence. Lawrence hoped to establish some sense of reassurance and order to what was left of the diminishing city. One of his first orders of business was the construction of a specially built booth, paneled with sturdy sheets of glass on all 4 sides. He spent all of his office hours sitting in this glass case. This way, he could serve the public and fend off the disease simultaneously.

Spearheaded by the Lord Mayor, the remaining authorities instituted a refined set of Plague Orders, colloquially referred to as the "Lord Mayor's Orders." These orders borrowed elements from past decrees such as Italy, a nation that has had more than plenty of experience with the plague. The orders were also upgraded with new regulations that satisfied the needs of the current situation. The compiled regulations were presented to the public on the 1st of July, but would only truly be enforced later that month.

To start with, Lawrence called for the aldermen to appoint at least 1-3 officials who were "of good sort and credit" to act as the "examiners" of each parish, a post that would be held for at least 2 months. Those who ditched their posts or refused to comply with duties assigned to them were imprisoned. Examiners were in charge of identifying and keeping tabs on infected households. They had the ability to order the provisional shut-in of suspicious households until the illness was officially diagnosed. If the ill displayed any symptoms, they were handed off to the constable to start the quarantine.

When a house had been rendered infected, a red cross was painted onto the doors of their homes, oftentimes, with the words "Lord have mercy upon us" scrawled on top of these symbols. Those who had come in contact with the diseased were required to wield dyed staffs at all times. More and more blacksmiths imposed themselves on infected homes, outfitting heavy-duty padlocks on their doors.

A pair of watchmen would also be posted outside the front doors of every infected household, working in alternating shifts around the clock. They would not only scope out potential intruders or absconders, they catered to all the food, drink, medical care, and other necessities of the sick. If the watchmen were to leave their post for any reason, they must double-check to ensure that the door has been bolted shut, and take the key with them. Those who failed to uphold their duties were either penalized or thrown behind bars. Likewise, unauthorized visitors who were discovered inside infected houses were forcefully locked in with the sick for a standard period of 40 days, with their release only permitted upon recovery. Needless to say, seeing daylight again was almost unheard of.

Women in the city were employed as "searchers." Searchers were the first to arrive on the scene and come in contact with the victims' corpses. They were a one-trick coroner of sorts, as their only job was to confirm the plague as the cause of death. Searchers often lodged together, but they were isolated from the rest of the public. Candidates were to be of "honest reputation," as these women vowed never to steal or take advantage of the deceased during their visits. Besides appointed physicians and nurses, the searchers were the only other people allowed in an infected household.

"Brokers of the dead" was a title given to those who visited these homes, scouring the place and corpse for money and other valuables. Profits derived from their sales were funneled back into the parish. The public funds were usually managed by the churchwarden or alderman, and its money used to purchase food, drink, and medication for the sick of the community.

In late July, the vacancy for grave diggers had doubled, as did the grisly specialty professions that nobody wanted. Under the mayor's orders, men from all over the city were rounded up and burdened with the slaughtering of 40,000 dogs and somewhere between 80,000 to 200,000 cats, to prevent the infection from spreading. Because these undesirable jobs required a strong stomach, they were compensated accordingly.

As the plague continued to spread, the mayor established a curfew for every parish. All taverns, inns, and other places of business or entertainment were to shut its doors by 9:00 p.m. every night. With time, the mayor's orders extended with more improved regulations. Gravediggers were to ensure that their graves were at least 6-feet deep, and all funerals and public gatherings prohibited.

The new regulations did not stop there. Fires were to be kept alight all 24 hours of the day, as it was believed to cleanse and purify the poisonous air. These fires were often scented with pepper and frankincense, which not only veiled the decay of the city but also acted as a disinfectant. Houses were ordered to be swept clean and scrubbed from top to bottom. The dumping of trash and waste outside homes and in the streets became punishable by law. Authorities also made sure to discipline those who broke into and out of the infected houses to steal from the infected and dead.

The awful morale at the time was unimaginable, but Lord Mayor Lawrence was applauded for his efficiency at keeping the public pantry fully stocked. London's remembrancer, who served as the medium of communication between the Lord Mayor and the public, praised his superior. He gushed, "Everything was managed with so much care and excellent order observed in the whole city, suburbs, that London may be a pattern and example to all cities of the world for the good government and excellent order that was everywhere kept even in the most violent infection and the people were in the utmost consternation and distress."

As driven as the mayor was, his critics deemed his laws overambitious, as they would prove difficult to enforce. Moreover, the deeper the plague penetrated, less were available to supervise all the infected houses at one time, and 18-20 watchmen were murdered at their posts. At times, the ill, driven to near madness from the forced and prolonged confinement, slipped a noose through the upper gap of the front door and lassoed it around the snoozing guard's neck, strangling him before breaking free.

What was more, even with all the measures set in place, as well as the admiration the mayor's determination had garnered from his peers, the number of plague-related deaths in London climbed. In the beginning of July, the death toll was at 267, but by the end of the month, that number had spiked to 2,020. Granted, Lawrence's supporters argued that the number would have been higher without the mayor's orders and safety tactics, but the morale was swiftly sinking all the same. It was an era of constant surveillance and vigilance.

Most of all, Londoners were clambering on top of one another to make it past the border, but they were hopelessly shackled. A month earlier, the mayor had barred the gates of the city shut. This was a controversial but necessary measure enacted to prevent London's infected residents from further spreading the disease to other cities. If one wanted to make it past that border, they would have to present a clean certificate of health. These certificates were commonly described as becoming "more valuable than gold." It was with this truth that a new side business was bred by forgers of the city, who produced counterfeit documents for those who could cough up the sum.

The mayor's worst fears had been realized. London's borders may have been closed, but the countless infected and counterfeit document holders who managed to escape spread the disease to nearby cities and towns anyway.

Around August of 1665, the plague had made its way to the village of Eyam in Derbyshire. Eyam was a small village that housed only 350 residents, headed by its parish and church leader, William Mompesson. That summer, a local tailor received a package of laundry from London. The tailor unwrapped the package and lurched back at once, retracting a hand crawling with ravenous fleas. He discarded the package, slapped at his hand repeatedly, and burnt the clothes as soon as he had a moment to spare, but the fleas had gotten the better of him. Within a week, the tailor was dead, found with an ugly boil peeking out from behind his collar.

By the end of September, 5 more in Eyam had died from the plague. In the next month, that number was raised to 23. As the deaths continued to escalate, the frightened villagers begged Mompesson for permission to flee to the plague-free Sheffield in northern England. With a heavy heart, Mompesson attempted to and succeeded in coaxing his villagers into staying so that the disease could be contained. Mompesson continued to preach, but his services were relocated outside of town to minimize the chance of infection to the flock, many of whom had come from nearby cities. Neighboring communities who learned of their heroism came to their aid. Food was left on the parish stones by the border of Eyam. Coins were also dropped into jars of vinegar next to these stones.

Eventually, up to 260 of Eyam's 350 inhabitants would waste away from the disease. Among the dead was Mompesson's wife. As for the preacher, he lived to see the plague run its course.

Therapy

"To the Exchange, where I have not been in a great while. But, 'Lord!' how sad a sight is to see streets empty of people. Jealous of every door that one sees shut... God preserve us all." – Samuel Pepys

Those who were left behind to defend themselves began to set up their own precautions. Almost every single inhabitant that had been abandoned in London was well below the poverty line, and their distress, along with the plague, was understandably thriving. After all, these people, as one historian put it, were the "human fuel for an epidemic."

The remaining Londoners worked to uphold the best sanitary standards their environment allowed them. Businessmen and merchants, like those who came to the aid of the villagers at Eyam, deposited coins into vinegar jars as a means of sterilization. Raw meat at butcher shops was no longer handled by hand but instead with hooks. Letters received from within or outside the city walls were intercepted by authorities, and all sealed documents were waved over the smoke arising from cauldrons of boiling vinegar before they were opened.

People taught their children to inspect themselves every night before bed, on the constant lookout for any buboes of visible symptoms. Apart from the bubo, which averaged about the size of a chicken egg, they searched for dark discoloration and swelling around the neck. More signs that alluded to any of the 3 strains of plague included fevers, chills, nausea, headaches, sudden fatigues, abdominal pain, diarrhea, vomiting, irregular bleeding, and gangrene in the nose, toes, or fingers.

Those who were responsible for caring for the diseased also took unique precautions of their own. One such example was the costume most plague physicians and nurses wore during the visits to the infected patients' homes. Since most believed and promoted the miasma theory, those giving care wore distinctive metal masks fitted with a long beak, the creation of a French doctor named Charles de Lorme in 1619. The beaks were packed with an aromatic blend of spices, herbs, and dried flowers to combat the foul odors, as well as the toxicity in the air. These masks, now often associated with the plague, were often paired with a waxen coat that covered one from head to toe for whole-body protection, completing the "beak doctor costume."

The absent physicians who sought refuge in the countryside began to roll out one publication after another containing cures and safeguards for the people back home, and as the outbreak intensified, more scholars and enterprising minds stepped forward with "educated" suggestions of their own. Among these publications was one assembled by the Royal College of Physicians, *For the Cure of the Plague, As for the Preventing of Infection.*

The wordily-titled guidebook, which presented precautions and advice on how to fumigate houses and articles of clothing, as well as natural scent-related remedies, concluded with a section of recipes. These recipes were split in 2 parts, one devoted to rich, and one for the poor.

Many of the well-received remedies for the "richer sort" involved the use of powdered unicorn horn and crushed emeralds. These false remedies, often advertised as "plague water," were a common scam employed by crooks of the time that pounced on the chance to swindle the frantic and weak-minded. Another recipe instructed the rich to ingest 3 grams of Laudanum a day; this opiate powder was to be stirred into brandy for good measure. The poor were offered solutions that cost little to nothing, such as arsenic amulets that could be worn around the neck or clamped under one's arms. 10-year-old treacle was taken as a plague-rejecting vitamin.

Recipes for pastes were also provided for women or children who preferred to avoid bitter-tasting remedies. One of these concoctions involved the grinding and mixing of rose petals, wood sorrel, sage flowers, wood syrup, harts-horn shavings, and more, which was to be coated on twice a day. Other recipes pertained to perfumes or portable scented satchels. One formula called for wormwood, myrrh, valerian, snake-root, and a variety of other hard-to-find herbs and roots.

As a method of pain relief, the rich often turned to fine wine and other agents to curb the intolerable agony. The poor turned to smoking tobacco, which at the time was commended for its healing and allegedly disease-deterring properties. Samuel Pepys was one of those who publicly advocated for this method, and he was known for chewing tobacco to keep himself free of the disease.

Children were no exception. In fact, they were encouraged to partake in these cures, and if they had the gall to refuse the pipe, they would often be beaten or disciplined by their guardians. As discussed in the account of a scholar from Eton, the year the plague reached its peak, all the boys in school were ordered to puff on a tobacco pipe every morning. Those that disobeyed were flogged. Children were also prescribed medicinal drinks that contained severe levels of alcohol and opium.

The surviving apothecaries of London were often sold out of the most bizarre cures and prophylactics, which also impacted the market. For instance, rosemary, a favored stench-masker, was previously priced at a shilling for a large sack. During the plague, that price jumped as high as 6 shillings for a meager handful.

The use of lucky charms was another doctor-endorsed measure. Dr. George Thomson, for one, was remembered for wearing a dead toad as a necklace. Another eccentric charm was a scroll of parchment tucked into the clothes of Londoners featuring the words "abracadabra," its letters written in triangular form. Others, following doctors' recommendations, sported a rabbit's foot or covered themselves with leeches.

Buboes were lanced and drained, and while it has now been concluded to be harmful and ineffective, it was seen as one of the only practical cures and pain relief techniques of the time. Fully-plucked chickens were then strapped onto the bubo or open sore, as people believed this transferred all the bacteria to the clucking and squirming animal. Another particularly dangerous cure was the consuming of arsenic and mercury syrups.

The church also chimed in, promoting a cure of their own – the power of prayer.

The Peak

"The sad news of the death of so many in the parish of the plague, 40 last night, the bell always going... either for deaths or burials." – Samuel Pepys

By August of 1665, the Bills of Mortality indicated that up to 7,000 victims a week were tagged with the plague as their cause of death. As a grave reminder, these were statistics that purely pertained to Christian parishes; the Jews, Quakers, Muslims, and other non-Christians across England went uncounted.

The facilities in London that were constructed to counter the plague were grossly insufficient when it came to serving the speedily rising numbers of the sick public. During the mass exodus of London's wealthy class, a nobleman and soldier, William, 1st Earl of Craven, chose to stay behind. Along with the Lord Mayor's orders, William called for the establishment of more pest houses, otherwise referred to as "plague houses," as well as the bulk burial of the deceased in enormous plague pits. As the plague continued to slither across the city, he hastily ordered the purchases of unused land, and transformed buildings into pest houses in Lancaster Gate, as well as the parishes of St. Clement Danes, St. Paul, St. James, and St. Martin-in-the-Fields. And yet, these pest houses could do nothing to dampen the fury of the plague.

Records from these pest houses have been clumsily misplaced by the hands of time. Therefore, modern experts have found it problematic to determine the extent of the effectiveness when it comes to these makeshift plague hospitals. Today, there are some who agree that the isolation of the sick in these establishments, albeit suffering extraordinarily substandard sanitary conditions, helped reduce the number of victims to a certain degree. On the other hand, there are those who argue that the rise in these forced quarantines and confinements in grungy and cramped spaces only helped to perpetuate the disease, and as such, was responsible for the lengthening of the Bills of Mortality. One scholar observed, "Infection may have killed its thousands, but shutting up have killed its ten-thousands."

Moreover, as these pest houses were privately owned and unregulated by the government, they earned a nasty reputation of their own. The condemnation of these pest houses repelled many from venturing through its front doors. Since the majority of doctors and trained physicians were nowhere to be found, most of the pest houses were staffed with only nurses, many of them vastly inexperienced. These nurses were also often uneducated and hired straight off the streets, no qualifications needed.

Perhaps unsurprisingly, despite the fact that these nurses had accepted a job no one dared touch with a 10-foot pole, the public's anger was often projected to these nurses, who were accused of further spreading the disease. The nurses soon found themselves surrounded by reputation-destructing hearsay, often unfounded. They were accused of scheming to murder their patients for ill-gotten gains. These "wretches," as many grew to call them, were supposedly strangling and suffocating their patients behind closed doors. Once the victim ceased their struggling, the nurses swooped in like gold-digging vultures and picked the corpse clean. Their greed was demonstrated through their recklessness in caring for the sick but unsettling shrewdness when it came to plundering their defenseless victims. Other nurses were accused of extracting "pestilential taint" from the bleeding sores of the sick. The goo was then allegedly bottled up, later to be secretly injected into the healthy, as a mode of shady but stable income. Regardless of the popularity of these warped narratives, records from Cock and Key Alley presented proof of a certain Nurse Fletcher that contradicted that stereotype. After stumbling upon valuables that amounted to more than a month's salary in one of the victim's homes, she reportedly returned every last shilling to the parish that same day.

Meanwhile, the restlessness among the trapped Londoners soared. Many vocally protested the policy of imprisoning all the occupants of an infected household, and they fought to find a way for uninfected occupants to flee before the clock ran out. Watchmen standing guard outside quarantined homes, along with guards by the city border, were often bribed by those seeking to escape, while others paid off officials to overlook plague symptoms in their homes. Some families were so hell-bent on fleeing that they left all their belongings and deserted their homes, choosing to live with nothing on the streets rather than risk permanent house arrest.

Those who were locked up in quarantine had to conjure up escape methods that required much more creativity. Other than the last-resort "fishing for guards" technique, which involved the use of a noose, some armed themselves with spoons, shovels, and other tools in an effort to tunnel their way out to freedom. Others attempted adrenaline-fueled rooftop escapes. There were also those who persuaded their friends to slip poison or sleep-inducing drugs into the watchmen's food to clear the coast.

Those at their wits' end set fire to their homes. A few hacked away at the weakest walls in their abodes but were almost always immediately tackled to the ground by the watchmen. In one incredible episode, a man attached a contraption made out of fireworks to his door and detonated the bomb, leaping out with his family through the window in the nick of time.

On the 12th of August, the Lord Mayor, who could no longer ignore the unremittingly plummeting morale, made a decisive attempt to bring back a sense of unity. For one night only, the healthy were ordered inside their homes by 9:00 p.m. to allow those that had been locked up outside of their homes for a few hours. The momentarily freed captives were swathed in thick cloths and scarves from head to toe so that they could experience the ephemeral "liberty of [going] abroad for air." That night, the physically fit peered out of their windows, watching as a mob of the zombie-like plague patients roamed the streets. While stepping outside would have meant joining the condemned, many were tempted to burst out of their homes and into the crowd, as some would have spotted loved ones they had not seen for close to a month. Even more heartbreaking, the faces detected were most likely those they would never see again.

By September of 1665, London's plague-related mortality rates saw yet another unwanted spike. Now, between 8,000-10,000 Londoners were dying each week. Gradually, circumstances devolved into such a sorry state that most municipal authorities had given up on enforcing the preventative measures they had worked so hard to promote. What was left of the watchmen no longer stood guard outside quarantined homes. Their duties were instead redirected to the handling of the dead.

Plague in 1665.

A depiction of corpses being buried in London in 1665

Communal burial pits became an equally chilling reality of the plague. These plague pits only multiplied, as bodies racked up faster than personal graves could be dug. The sight of "plague carts" driving up and down the streets of London became routine. The drivers of these harrowing death vehicles were often heard crying out to the public, "Bring out your dead!"

At first, authorities worried that the number of bodies would add to the alarm of an already disconcerted public, so the Lord Mayor ordered for all plague pit burials to be scheduled after curfew hours. This policy was altered not long after when authorities realized that doing so had cut the precious burial time in half. This would not do, as this meant that the stacks of decomposing bodies, including those of children, in infected households, streets, and alleys, which were quickly piling up, would be left unattended. Once again, drivers of plague carts resumed their daytime duties.

During the outbreak's worst phases, these drivers dumped entire carts of bodies into these pits, all at once, to save time. The Aldgate parish featured one of the largest plague pits, stretching 50-feet long and 20-feet wide, said to fit over 1,100 corpses. Other plague sites around London included the parishes of St. Bride's, Finsbury Fields, Goswell Street, Golden Square in Soho, and several in the St. Dunstan area.

Those who dreamt of fleeing saw their wills strained until their conviction ultimately fizzled out. The church bells that signaled the death of a victim rang for hours on end, until the mere act of tolling the bell no longer made sense. Continuing to do so would have required a new man for the post, a full-time commitment at that.

At this stage of the outbreak, those who were left were hollow shells of their past selves. To put matters in perspective, the loved ones who had dropped dead around the average Londoner either amounted to or surpassed the number and heartache that would have been otherwise distributed over a lifetime. More than ever, it became easier for them to latch onto theories that might have seemed downright ludicrous in a different setting.

A dubious theory from Paris soon crossed London's borders. Word began to spread that diseases such as pox or syphilis, the latter a highly contagious sexually transmitted disease, could make one immune to the plague. This rumor prompted the healthy to frequent brothels for easy access to the STD. Some of the infected paid for sex with prostitutes in the hopes of replacing one poison with a lesser disease that came with a better chance of survival. Another myth supported by dicey medieval science asserted that diseases, including the plague, could be erased through intercourse with a virgin of either gender. Consequently, this resulted in an increase in underage victims.

Towards the end of 1665, the Bills of Mortality published a total of 68,594 plague deaths in its

London registry. Experts believe that these figures have also been seriously distorted over the years because the leading causes of death that followed were suspected to have been associated with the plague. Among the other leading causes were 4,664 who died of "fever," 3,173 to "consumption," (a retired term for tuberculosis),1,855 to "spotted fever," (also known as meningitis or typhus), and finally, 1,931 to "teething," which referred to toddlers who died during or before the completion of their teething stage.

A Storm Weathered and a Winter's Thaw

"'Should evil come upon us, the sword, or judgment, or pestilence, or famine, we will stand before this house and before You (for your name is in this house) and cry to You in our distress, and You will hear and deliver us.'" – 2 Chronicles 20:9

Even with the patent fire hazards that came with the fumigation process, the trend began to catch on. Fumigation was championed by the officials of London, a practice proposed by one James Angier. Back in June, Angier had managed to persuade the Privy Council into allowing him to conduct an experiment of his own to test out the process. The trials transpired in a ramshackle house in Newton Street, close to Holborn. Of the 12 occupants in the residence, 4 had already expired from the plague, while 2 of the remaining 8 showed hints of the disease.

The fumigation process entailed the burning of a medley of saltpeter (another term for potassium nitrate), amber, and brimstone. The stupendous stench caused by the burning of these materials was said to have been so profound that it drove off all the rodents, fleas, and pests from a household. As the experiment concluded, there were no more recorded deaths in the post-fumigated home.

When King Charles II learned of the vigorous acclamation surrounding Angier's pioneering germicide techniques, he demanded for all the structures within London to undergo this treatment. Tremendous shipments of coal were purchased for the daunting task. The coal would be used to kindle giant, crackling fires that would serve as fumigants for every 6 houses. As the clouds of smoke, steeped in the fragrance of sweet herbs, swirled over the city, Londoners were filled with renewed hope. It seemed as if the city of London could be saved, after all.

Regrettably, this sense of hope soon tapered off when the weather experienced a sudden mood swing. The thundering skies turned gray, its tears dousing the flames across the city. When the skies eventually cleared, the citizens of London dragged themselves out of their shelters and went to work on resuscitating the flames.

Slowly but surely, it appeared as if the winter of 1665 had once again erected a roadblock against the disease. As the Bills of Mortality continued to shrink, those who had decamped began their cautious trek back home. Some of those who had returned, perhaps in some way racked with the guilt of their departure, began to look after the ill.

Sadly, the immune systems of a large number of these returning refugees failed to combat the ghastly plague, making them highly susceptible to the disease. They soon fell victim to their newly contracted infections, contributing to the brief rise in the death toll in December of 1665. Luckily for London, this proved to be no more than a deceptive glint in the pan, and in the weeks that followed, the plague began to wane. The intervals between Bills of Mortality updates grew longer and longer.

When February of 1666 rolled around, the outbreak was officially declared dormant. That same month, the king and his family, along with the justices, court officials, and members of Parliament, returned to the city. While Parliament had returned, the governing body would not be formally reinstated until September that year. By the following month's end, Edward Hyde, the Lord Chancellor and 1st Earl of Clanderon, summarized the resolution of the revived city in a letter, writing that "the streets were as full, the exchange as much crowded, and the people, in all places as numerous, as they had ever been, few persons missing any of their acquaintance..."

Under the command of Parliament's Rebuilding of London Act 1666, business picked up where it had left off. Trade resumed. The boards to quarantined homes were prised off, the structures dismantled, and rebuilt. Shops and places of entertainment reopened their doors. The cragged and damaged roads in the central areas of London were stripped and repaved with smoother and wider streets. New sewage systems were developed to help boost the city's sanitation standards. This was a project that would take over a decade to complete, headed by Robert Hooke, the Surveyor of London.

In May of that year, the Privy Council of the city reinstituted a revised version of the plague orders, prohibiting the burial of future plague-stricken corpses in churchyards. The council also required its residents to use quicklime – cement or mortar produced by heating limestone – in approved burial sites. None of these graves were to be disturbed for a minimum of 1 year, as this helped to ensure that the disease could no longer be contracted by anyone coming into contact with these corpses.

The outbreak might have been declared obsolete, but in the months that followed, a few cases of plague-related deaths popped up intermittently across the nation. These periodic cases would appear in the mid-summer of 1666, up until the last-ever outbreak-related case in 1669.

As 1666 carried on, it seemed as if things could only go better from there, but Londoners were sorely mistaken. On the 2nd of September, a fire erupted in King's Bakery in Pudding Lane, close to the fabled London Bridge. Fires were a relatively common occurrence during the time, but the "tinder-dry" and uncharacteristically rain-less heat allowed the fire to proliferate almost effortlessly. An estimated 300 structures were said to have been burned to the ground before the fire was finally extinguished 4 days later. Still and all, there were those that saw a silver lining in the catastrophe; some came to believe that the disastrous fire had been the key to stamping out the plague in London once and for all. Today, modern historians believe that the plague had already tapered off before the disaster, and by the time it was gone, an estimated 100,000 Londoners had died in less than 16 months.

Theories aimed at determining what caused the end of the outbreaks that claimed over 200 million people by the end of its run continue to surface to this day. Some say it was the fumigation, quarantine, and other preventative measures that did away with the plague. Others contend that it had been the consistent improvements in personal hygiene in the years that followed. A definitive theory has yet to be found. How the "super survivors" of the plague, particularly those that never left London, could have built such an immunity, is another mystery that has yet to be solved.

In recent years, new findings have come forth concerning the cause of the plague itself, leading to some historians backtracking on previous prevailing theories. Back in 2001, scholars from Liverpool University suggested that the plague might have been caused by a virus much like Ebola, as opposed to the *yersinia pestis* bacterium. That same year, historian Norman Cantor proposed that the plague had been the result of anthrax, citing the anthrax spores found in Scotland during the time.

In 2015, scientists around the world fought to refute the theory that the plague had been manufactured by rats. For a time, gerbils were put on the hot seat, but that hypothesis was quickly put to rest. In September of the next year, tests from Germany confirmed the presence of the *yersinia pestis* bacterium from samples that had been found at an excavation site in Liverpool Street.

The horrors of the plague may seem like nothing more than a foul and fickle fiend of yesteryear, but this is a foe that can never be fully vanquished. Even now, an average of 7 plague cases are still reported each year in the United States alone.

Online Resources

Other books about English history by Charles River Editors

Other books about the Great Plague of London on Amazon

Bibliography

Contributors, Harvard University Library. "The Great Plague of London, 1665." *Harvard University Library*. The President and Fellows of Harvard College, 2008. Web. 27 Mar. 2017. <http://ocp.hul.harvard.edu/contagion/plague.html>.

Ross, David. "The London Plague of 1665." *The London Plague of 1665*. David Ross, 2010. Web. 27 Mar. 2017. <http://www.britainexpress.com/History/plague.htm>.

Editors, UK National Archives. "Great Plague of 1665-1666." *The National Archives*. The

National Archives Kew, Richmond, Surrey, 2015. Web. 27 Mar. 2017. <http://www.nationalarchives.gov.uk/education/resources/great-plague/>.

Stanbridge, Nicola. "DNA confirms cause of 1665 London's Great Plague." *BBC News*. BBC, 8 Sept. 2016. Web. 27 Mar. 2017. <http://www.bbc.com/news/science-environment-37287715>.

Fenn, Chris, Katy Stoddard, Apple Chan-Fardel, and Paul Torpey. "Mapping London's great plague of 1665." *The Guardian*. Guardian News and Media, Ltd., 12 Aug. 2015. Web. 27 Mar. 2017. <https://www.theguardian.com/society/ng-interactive/2015/aug/12/london-great-plague-1665-bills-of-mortality>.

Editors, BBC. "The Great Plague." *BBC Bitesize*. BBC, 2016. Web. 27 Mar. 2017. <http://www.bbc.co.uk/education/guides/zd3wxnb/revision/2>.

Authors, Snopes. "Ring Around the Rosie." *Snopes*. Proper Media, 12 July 2015. Web. 27 Mar. 2017. <http://www.snopes.com/language/literary/rosie.asp>.

Smallwood, Karl. "TOADS AROUND YOUR NECK AND FORCING KIDS TO SMOKE-ESCAPING THE GREAT PLAGUE OF LONDON (1665-1666)." *Today I Found Out*. Today I Found Out, 27 May 2015. Web. 27 Mar. 2017. <http://www.todayifoundout.com/index.php/2015/05/great-plague-london/>.

Authors, The Black Death. "How does the nursery rhyme "Ring around the Rosie" Relate to the Black Death?" *The Black Death*. Blogspot, 17 May 2011. Web. 27 Mar. 2017. <http://theblackdeathkc.blogspot.tw/2011/05/how-does-nursery-rhyme-ring-around.html>.

Schladweiler, Jon. "The history of a nursery rhyme — Ring around the Rosie." *The History of Sanitary Sewers*. WordPress, 19 Feb. 2002. Web. 27 Mar. 2017. <http://www.sewerhistory.org/miscellaneous/the-history-of-a-nursery-rhyme-ring-around-the-rosie/>.

Benedictow, Ole J. "The Black Death: The Greatest Catastrophe Ever." *History Today*. History Today, Ltd., 3 Mar. 2005. Web. 27 Mar. 2017. <http://www.historytoday.com/ole-j-benedictow/black-death-greatest-catastrophe-ever>.

Stöppler, Melissa Conrad, MD. "Plague (Black Death)." *MedicineNet*. Ed. Steven Doerr. MedicineNet, Inc., 8 Oct. 2015. Web. 27 Mar. 2017. <http://www.medicinenet.com/plague_facts/article.htm>.

Editors, Healthline. "The Plague." *Healthline*. Healthline Media, 2016. Web. 27 Mar. 2017. <http://www.healthline.com/health/plague#Overview1>.

Authors, History Channel. "BLACK DEATH." *History Channel.* A&E Television Networks, LLC, 2015. Web. 27 Mar. 2017. <http://www.history.com/topics/black-death>.

Snell, Melissa. "The Spread of the Black Death through Europe." *Thought Company.* About, Inc., 13 Jan. 2017. Web. 27 Mar. 2017. <https://www.thoughtco.com/spread-of-the-black-death-through-europe-4123214>.

Hope, Jessica. "10 things you (probably) didn't know about the Black Death." *History Extra.* Immediate Media Company, 2 Nov. 2015. Web. 27 Mar. 2017. <http://www.historyextra.com/article/international-history/10-things-you-probably-didnt-know-about-black-death>.

Newman, Simon. "The Black Death." *The Finer Times.* The Finer Times, 8 Oct. 2014. Web. 28 Mar. 2017. <http://www.thefinertimes.com/Middle-Ages/the-black-death.html>.

Wheelis, Mark. "Biological Warfare at the 1346 Siege of Caffa." *Centers for Disease Control and Prevention.* CDC Media, 16 July 2010. Web. 28 Mar. 2017. <https://wwwnc.cdc.gov/eid/article/8/9/01-0536_article>.

Steve, Rick. "The Plague That Shook Medieval Europe." *Rick Steve's Europe.* Rick Steves' Europe, Inc., 2017. Web. 28 Mar. 2017. <https://www.ricksteves.com/watch-read-listen/read/articles/the-plague-that-shook-medieval-europe>.

Editors, SHSU. "Boccaccio describes the Plague in Florence in the Introduction of the Decameron." *Sam Houston State University.* Sam Houston State University, 2003. Web. 28 Mar. 2017. <http://www.shsu.edu/~his_ncp/Boccaccio.html>.

Pearce, Ian. "Black Death." *Great Ayton.* Great Ayton, May 2009. Web. 28 Mar. 2017. <http://greatayton.wdfiles.com/local--files/public-health/Black-Death.pdf>.

Editors, AF. "The plague in Milan." *Archivum Fabricae.* Veneranda Fabbrica del Duomo di Milano, Feb. 2015. Web. 28 Mar. 2017. <http://archivio.duomomilano.it/en/infopage/the-plague-in-milan/bfa2bcc5-5bbc-4729-9181-46f6646bece7/>.

Authors, Museum of London. "London Plagues 1348-1665." *Museum of London.* Museum of London, 2013. Web. 28 Mar. 2017. <https://www.museumoflondon.org.uk/application/files/5014/5434/6066/london-plagues-1348-1665.pdf>.

Williams, Chris. "ANATOMY OF A FLEA BITE." *Colonial Pest Control.* Colonial Pest Control, Inc., 11 Sept. 2014. Web. 28 Mar. 2017. <http://www.colonialpest.com/anatomy-of-a-flea-bite/>.

Authors, Sunday Times. "The novice's study." *Sunday Times*. Wijeya Newspapers, Ltd., 2006. Web. 28 Mar. 2017. <http://www.sundaytimes.lk/060702/plus/PlusP4.1.html>.

Editors, Stone Age Refugee. "How many valiant men..." *Stone Age Refugee*. WordPress, 24 Mar. 2011. Web. 28 Mar. 2017. <https://stoneagerefugee.wordpress.com/2011/03/24/how-many-valiant-men-how-many-fair-ladies-breakfast-with-their-kinfolk-and-the-same-night-supped-with-their-ancestors-in-the-next-world-the-condition-of-the-people-was-pitiable-to-behold-they-sick/>.

Frith, John. "The History of Plague – Part 1. The Three Great Pandemics." *Journal of Military and Veterans' Health*. Australasian Military Medicine Association, 4 Feb. 2012. Web. 28 Mar. 2017. <http://jmvh.org/article/the-history-of-plague-part-1-the-three-great-pandemics/>.

DNews. "Bubonic Plague Originated in China." *Seeker*. Group Nine Media, 1 Nov. 2010. Web. 28 Mar. 2017. <https://www.seeker.com/bubonic-plague-originated-in-china-1765135886.html>.

Walker, Cameron. "Bubonic Plague Traced to Ancient Egypt." *National Geographic News*. National Geographic Society, 10 Mar. 2004. Web. 28 Mar. 2017. <http://news.nationalgeographic.com/news/2004/03/0310_040310_blackdeath.html>.

Authors, Telegraph. "Medieval London: 10 disgusting facts." *The Telegraph*. Telegraph Media Group, Ltd., 5 Apr. 2011. Web. 29 Mar. 2017. <http://www.telegraph.co.uk/culture/tvandradio/8421415/Medieval-London-10-disgusting-facts.html>.

Kollenborn, K. P. "15 Medieval Hygiene Practices That Might Make You Queasy." *K.P.Kollenborn*. Blogspot, 9 Jan. 2015. Web. 29 Mar. 2017. <http://kpkollenborn.blogspot.tw/2014/11/15-medieval-hygiene-practices-that.html>.

Richter, Ash M. "13 Gross Medieval Hygiene Practices That Will Give You Nightmares." *All Day*. All Day, 2015. Web. 29 Mar. 2017. <http://www.allday.com/13-gross-medieval-hygiene-practices-that-will-give-you-nightmares-2180807051.html>.

Authors, GSSG. "Life in a Medieval Town." *Go Social Studies Go*. Wix, 2008. Web. 29 Mar. 2017. <http://www.gohistorygo.com/medieval-towns->.

Brown, Stephanie. "What did medieval people think caused the Black Death, and how did they respond accordingly?" *Gorffennol Student Journal*. British Conference of Undergraduate Research, Winter 2007. Web. 29 Mar. 2017. <http://gorffennol.swansea.ac.uk/wp-content/uploads/2016/01/2-Black-Death.pdf>.

Banks-Smith, Nancy. "Dead reckoning ." *The Guardian*. Guardian News and Media, Ltd., 16 Oct. 2001. Web. 29 Mar. 2017.
<https://www.theguardian.com/media/2001/oct/16/tvandradio.television1>.

Conlon, Katherine. "The Plague Pits of London." *Travel Darkly*. Travel Darkly, Ltd., 23 Apr. 2014. Web. 29 Mar. 2017. <http://www.traveldarkly.com/plague-pits-london/>.

Editors, Encyclopedia.Com. "Bills Of Mortality." *Encyclopedia.Com*. The Gale Group, Inc., 2002. Web. 30 Mar. 2017. <http://www.encyclopedia.com/history/modern-europe/british-and-irish-history/bills-mortality>.

Johnson, Ben. "The Great Plague." *Historic UK*. Historic UK, Ltd., 4 Jan. 2013. Web. 30 Mar. 2017. <http://www.historic-uk.com/HistoryUK/HistoryofEngland/The-Great-Plague/>.

Mason, Emma. "London's 7 most memorable lord mayors." *History Extra*. Immediate Media Company, 5 Sept. 2016. Web. 30 Mar. 2017.
<http://www.historyextra.com/article/feature/london-lord-mayors-history-7-most-memorable>.

Trueman, C. N. "The Lord Mayor's Orders." *The History Learning Site*. The History Learning Site, Ltd., 17 Mar. 2015. Web. 30 Mar. 2017.
<http://www.historylearningsite.co.uk/stuart-england/the-lord-mayors-orders/>.

Trueman, C. N. "Eyam and the Great Plague of 1665." *The History Learning Site*. The History Learning Site, Ltd., 16 Aug. 2016. Web. 30 Mar. 2017.
<http://www.historylearningsite.co.uk/stuart-england/eyam-and-the-great-plague-of-1665/>.

Staff, Mayo Clinic. "Symptoms and causes." *Mayo Clinic*. Mayo Foundation for Medical Education and Research, 15 Mar. 2016. Web. 30 Mar. 2017.
<http://www.mayoclinic.org/diseases-conditions/plague/symptoms-causes/dxc-20196766>.

White, Frances. "Why did doctors during the Black Death wear 'beak masks'?" *History Answers*. Imagine Publishing Media, 2 June 2014. Web. 30 Mar. 2017.
<https://www.historyanswers.co.uk/people-politics/why-did-doctors-during-the-black-death-wear-beak-masks/>.

Birkwood, Katie. "For the cure of the plague." *Royal College of Physicians*. The Royal College of Physicians of London, 15 May 2015. Web. 30 Mar. 2017.
<https://www.rcplondon.ac.uk/news/cure-plague>.

Editors, RCP. "Plague remedies from the garden." *Royal College of Physicians*. The Royal College of Physicians of London, 4 Aug. 2015. Web. 30 Mar. 2017.
<https://www.rcplondon.ac.uk/news/plague-remedies-garden>.

Smith, Lisa. "Tag: Pest House Fields." *The Sloane Letters Project*. University of Saskatchewan , 15 Mar. 2013. Web. 30 Mar. 2017. <http://sloaneletters.com/tag/pest-house-fields/>.

Shariff, Mohammed. "10 Crazy Cures for the Black Death." *Listverse*. Listverse, Ltd., 21 Jan. 2013. Web. 31 Mar. 2017. <http://listverse.com/2013/01/21/10-crazy-cures-for-the-black-death/>.

Johnson, Ben. "The Great Fire of London." *Historic UK*. Historic UK, Ltd., 3 Sept. 2016. Web. 31 Mar. 2017. <http://www.historic-uk.com/HistoryUK/HistoryofEngland/The-Great-Fire-of-London/>.

Authors, The Week. "What was Black Death and how did it end?" *The Week*. The Week, Ltd., 31 Aug. 2016. Web. 31 Mar. 2017. <http://www.theweek.co.uk/76088/what-was-black-death-and-how-did-it-end>.

Morelle, Rebecca. "'Gerbils replace rats' as main cause of Black Death." *BBC News*. BBC, 24 Feb. 2015. Web. 31 Mar. 2017. <http://www.bbc.com/news/science-environment-31588671>.

Editors, Wikipedia. "Theories of the Black Death." *Wikpedia*. Wikimedia Foundation, Inc., 1 Mar. 2017. Web. 31 Mar. 2017. <https://en.wikipedia.org/wiki/Theories_of_the_Black_Death#Ebola-like_virus>.

Creighton, Charles. *A History of Epidemics in Britain: From AD 664 to the Extinction of Plague*. Vol. 1. N.p.: Cambridge U Press, 2013. Print.

Hughes, Robert. *Barcelona*. N.p.: Vintage, 1993. Print.

Gill, John. *Andalucia: A Cultural History (Landscapes of the Imagination)*. N.p.: Oxford U Press, 2008. Print.

Porter, Stephen. *The Great Plague*. N.p.: Sutton Pub Ltd, 2000. Print.

Hays, Jo N. *Epidemics and Pandemics: Their Impacts on Human History*. 1st ed. N.p.: ABC-CLIO, 2005. Print.

Stone, Jon R. *The Routledge Dictionary of Latin Quotations: The Illiterati's Guide to Latin Maxims, Mottoes, Proverbs, and Sayings (Latin for the Illiterati)*. Bilingual ed. N.p.: Routledge, 2004. Print.

Gaskill, Malcolm. *Witchfinders: A Seventeenth-Century English Tragedy*. N.p.: Harvard U Press, 2007. Print.

Jones, Becky, and Clare Lewis. *The Bumper Book of London: Everything You Need to Know*

About London and More... . N.p.: Frances Lincoln, 2012. Print.

Moote, A. Lloyd, and Dorothy C. Moote. *The Great Plague: The Story of London's Most Deadly Year* . 1st ed. N.p.: Johns Hopkins U Press, 2006. Print.

Wright, Cindy. *The Dark Traveller*. N.p.: Lulu.Com, 2012. Print.

Withington, John. *London's Disasters: From Boudicca to the Banking Crisis*. N.p.: The History Press, 2010. Print.

Hayden, Deborah. *Pox: Genius, Madness, And The Mysteries Of Syphilis*. Reprint ed. N.p.: Basic , 2003. Print.

Hyde, Edward. *The History of the Rebellion and Civil Wars in England Begun in the Year 1641: (History of the Rebellion & Civil Wars in England Begun in the Year 1641)* . Ed. W. Dunn Macray. Vol. 5. N.p.: Clarendon Press, 1993. Print.

Appleby, Andrew B. *The Disappearance of Plague: A Continuing Puzzle*. N.p.: Economic History Society, 1980. Print.

N.p. "The Great Plague." *Plague, Fire, War and Treason: A Century of Troubles*. Channel 4. London, 31 Oct. 2005. Television.

Oliver, Dan. "Secrets of the Great Plague ." *Secrets of the Great Plague*. Dir. Tom Pollock. Atlantic Productions See. 28 Aug. 2006. Television.

Free Books by Charles River Editors

We have brand new titles available for free most days of the week. To see which of our titles are currently free, click on this link.

Discounted Books by Charles River Editors

We have titles at a discount price of just 99 cents everyday. To see which of our titles are currently 99 cents, click on this link.

Made in the USA
Las Vegas, NV
19 February 2025

18404665R00030